Getting Started in Fiction Editing

Second edition

Katherine Trail with Rachel Rowlands

First published in the UK in 2024 by
Chartered Institute of Editing and Proofreading
Studio 206, Milton Keynes Business Centre
Foxhunter Drive, Linford Wood
Milton Keynes
Buckinghamshire
MK14 6GD

ciep.uk

Copyright © 2024 Chartered Institute of Editing and Proofreading

ISBN 978 1 915141 21 7 (print)
ISBN 978 1 915141 22 4 (PDF ebook)
ISBN 978 1 915141 23 1 (ePub)

Second edition 2024

First edition 2018: ISBN 978 0 993129 34 6 (print), ISBN 978 0 993129 35 3 (PDF ebook)
Revised first edition 2020: ISBN 978 1 916148 12 3 (print), ISBN 978 1 916138 13 0 (PDF ebook)

All rights reserved. No part of this publication may be reproduced or used in any manner without written permission from the publisher, except for quoting brief passages in a review.

The moral rights of the authors have been asserted.

The information in this work is accurate and current at the time of publication to the best of the authors' and publisher's knowledge, but it has been written as a short summary or introduction only. Readers are advised to take further steps to ensure the correctness, sufficiency or completeness of this information for their own purposes.

Typeset in-house
Original design by Ave Design (avedesignstudio.com)
Image credits: Creative Commons from Unsplash and Pixabay

Contents

1	Introduction	1
2	Different kinds of editing	3
	Working for publishers	6
	Working for independent authors	7
3	The bones of the story	10
	Plot	10
	Scenes and structure	12
	Conflict and tension	12
	Point of view	13
	Pace	14
	Characterisation	15
	Showing vs telling	16
	Dialogue	17
	Tense times	17
	Author voice	19
	Series	19
4	Copyediting	21
	Style sheets	22
	Timelines	23
	Consistency	24
	Punctuating dialogue	25
	Inner monologue and thoughts	26
	Fact-checking	27

	Anachronisms	27
	Avoiding over-correction	28
	Repetition and redundancy	29
	Dealing with numbers	30
	Copyright and legal concerns	30
	Genre concerns	32
	Target audience	32
	Conscious language	33
	Document formatting	34
	Efficiency tools	35
	Macros	35
	Add-ins	36
	Text expanders	36
5 |	Resources	37
	Books	37
	Blogs and websites	38
6 |	Glossary	40

1 | Introduction

Editing fiction has much in common with editing non-fiction. In general, a good fiction editor needs to have the same eye for detail, the same love for and knowledge of language, and the same commitment to ensuring a positive and satisfying experience for the reader. However, a good fiction editor also needs to understand the art of writing: the importance of author voice; how to differentiate between author style and mistakes; and, perhaps most importantly, how to communicate changes sensitively. After all, a novel is most likely a labour of love. The author has probably dreamed of publishing their novel for years – and could well have taken years to write it. As fiction editors, it is up to us to carefully guide our clients through the various pitfalls and potholes on the road to publication.

Fiction editing starts with a love of reading and of books. So much of the knowledge needed for fiction editing comes from having experienced a huge variety of different genres and authors. When you read a book, you know if the story is good and engaging. You also know when it's not. Sometimes you might not be able to pinpoint exactly *why* something jars in the text, but you know something's wrong. That innate sense of understanding what makes a good story is something that can't be solely taught; it's something that someone who loves language and books learns on their journey through life.

This guide is an introduction to fiction editing. Its aim is to give the budding fiction editor some practical insight into how to work on fiction, be it for a publisher or for an independent author who is planning to self-publish or submit their work traditionally. It will also be useful for proofreaders who are interested in working on fiction.

"It's important to know what you can and can't offer an author."

2 | Different kinds of editing

The phrase 'fiction editing' spans a wide range of services and levels of intervention. Developmental editing, structural editing, substantive editing, content editing, line editing, copyediting, proof-editing, proofreading, manuscript assessments ... With so many different levels of editing, it's easy to see how clients might become overwhelmed. It doesn't help that some of the editorial stages can overlap, depending on how an editor approaches the work, so terminology and descriptions can vary quite substantially. In many respects, what you call a specific type of editing doesn't matter; the important thing is that your client knows exactly what to expect.

Some authors need help with the foundations of their story: plot, characterisation, pacing, narrative arc, point of view, etc. These authors won't be well served by a copyedit or proofread, both of which focus on word- and sentence-level matters. Authors who need this type of help are looking for what is variously called a developmental edit, a structural edit or a substantive edit. This often involves a hands-on approach to the text, where an editor will make extensive comments and

suggestions throughout a manuscript on how to resolve problems with the foundations of the story. While copyediting concerns might be noted, the editor's focus is on making the story satisfying.

A critique, manuscript appraisal or assessment, which usually takes the form of a written report, is a good option for authors who prefer less hands-on involvement. It can be helpful to authors who are more experienced in receiving feedback, and are confident in their abilities to implement it. The length of the written report can vary depending on the editor – these can be short and to-the-point, or long and extensive.

It is worth noting that the processes around these developmental services can be as varied as the naming conventions. Some editors offer telephone consultations alongside them, or a round of follow-up reads on revisions – others don't. One editor may offer short manuscript appraisals with a few pages of notes, whereas another will do exhaustive notes and pull out examples from the text. There is no right or wrong way to do a developmental edit, so long as both editor and writer agree about what the service involves.

Some authors might be happy with the structure and overall shape of their story but need some help to tidy up the language ahead of publication. A developmental edit isn't going to address those needs, but a line edit, a copyedit or a proofread will. Line editing is often seen as a heavier version of copyediting – focusing on stylistic issues and the art of writing as well as on the traditional copyediting concerns. There is always debate about these definitions, as freelance editors describe their services differently; some editors may not even distinguish between the two.

Tip
- As a rough rule of thumb, an author who has had no editorial intervention up until now is unlikely to need just a proofread. A light copyedit at the very least would be a common option, with a heavy copyedit or a line edit more likely, particularly for a novice author.

Working out which of these services serves the client best can be difficult. Authors tend to be most familiar with the term 'proofreading', but don't let that guide you down a wrong path as authors sometimes don't know the finer details of what these services involve.

If you're struggling with how to name and define your services, think about the types of clients you hope to work for. If you'll be working mainly with publishing houses, the definitions of proofreading and copyediting will be understood by your client. When working with indie authors, consider keeping things as clear as possible (eg, a light versus heavy copyedit, or a copyedit versus a line edit), and make sure you explain what's involved in your service. Whatever you decide to call the editing services you perform, and whatever level of intervention you choose, it is vital that the client understands what they are getting. It can be useful to carry out a sample edit, either for free or for a small sum, of a section of their book (a thousand words is a good amount) so they can see what kind of editing you offer. It's also helpful for you so you can estimate how long their book will take to edit as well as get a feel for how the author responds to your edits and queries. For some services (such as a critique or manuscript appraisal), it won't be feasible for you to perform a sample edit, so be sure to communicate clearly with the author about what the service would involve. Another option could be to offer paid opening chapter critiques to give uncertain writers a taster of what a full appraisal might involve, before they commit to having their full manuscript looked at.

There's also no shame in only offering copyediting or specialising in developmental editing. Every editor has their own strengths. If you feel out of your depth with a piece of work, then there are guaranteed to be other editors who would thrive on that type of material. It's important to know what you can and can't offer an author. Being able to say no and pass the work on elsewhere is a sign of a good editor. You can refer an author to the CIEP directory or post a message on the Marketplace forum (with the author's permission).

Working for publishers

When working for a publisher, they will tell you what kind of edit you should perform (such as a copyedit), and they'll be familiar with all the terminology, so there's no need to worry about communicating with the client about what the service involves. You'll also receive the publisher's own style guide to work with. By the time the work reaches you for a copyedit, it should be in good shape and not have major developmental issues or other problems. This isn't always the case, though, particularly for very small or new publishers who are still finding their way and learning the process themselves. If you do spot major issues with a piece of publisher work, it's best to let the desk editor know as soon as possible so they can decide what to do.

Publisher work has the advantage of being more self-contained than working with independent authors in the sense that, once the job is finished, it goes back to the publisher and your involvement is over. You don't have to deal with a nervous or worried author's questions about the publishing process. It also means that you're unlikely to have to make tough decisions about whether something is ready for editing; the publisher has already decided it is worth pursuing, and it's no doubt been through various editorial stages before it arrives in your inbox.

> ### Tip
> - Most importantly, stick to the brief. Unlike independent authors, who might not know what the difference between a copyedit and a proofread is, publishers usually know exactly what they are asking for. If they've asked for a quick proofread then that should be what you deliver – avoid the temptation to show off your training or knowledge by making other changes, unless explicitly asked to do so.

Sometimes you will be able to liaise directly with the author to resolve queries; other times you will have to go through the desk editor or managing editor. Just remember in your comments and emails to always be professional. You might think you're sending an offhand comment to a desk editor you have a good relationship with, only to have the email forwarded to the author for checking, and thereby causing offence. Assume that anyone at any level may read your comments or correspondence.

Getting work with large traditional publishers such as Bloomsbury, Macmillan, Penguin Random House or HarperCollins can be difficult as they tend to have a lot of editors who are keen to work with them already on their books. Sometimes it's worth setting your sights a bit more realistically at first; there are a lot of small, independent publishers in the UK and elsewhere who need freelance editors and/or proofreaders for their clients' books. Be aware that smaller publishers and independent presses often pay significantly less than larger ones (although this isn't always the case). You may want to decide how much of this type of work you'd like to do in order to get your foot in the door.

Have a look in the *Writers' and Artists' Yearbook*, published by Bloomsbury annually, to find out the names and contact details of publishers whose work you might find interesting. If you are keen to work with children's books, you can also consult the *Children's Writers' and Artists' Yearbook*, also published annually. Alternatively, instead of the physical yearbook, you can purchase a subscription to their online listings directory to get access to the same content.

Working for independent authors

Independent (indie) or self-publishing authors are a large part of the market for fiction editors today. There used to be a stigma around self-publishing, with the suggestion it was the domain of those who were unable to get a publishing deal. However, while this may be true for some authors, for many it is a conscious decision to be in control of their own destiny. Successful self-publishers like Mark Dawson, Joanna Penn and Amanda Hocking have made a business out of their writing, becoming excellent marketers and assembling a team of editors, proofreaders, cover designers and typesetters to put out books that are indistinguishable from traditionally published books.

Often, these are the same editors, proofreaders, cover designers and typesetters who also work freelance for traditional publishers. Through the work of organisations like the Alliance of Independent Authors, writers are realising the value of proper editing and putting out a professional product.

When embarking on a project with an independent author, there are some things to bear in mind. If the author is a novice, they may be unaware of how the editing process works – or even how the publishing process works in general. Be prepared to spend some time explaining your methods and answering their questions – you may want to work this into the quote for your service, if the author will need additional guidance. Authors can be quite apprehensive about handing over their work – which might only have been read by friends and family so far – to an editor and might even be embarrassed. This is where it's important to have empathy and sensitivity.

While self-publishing gives everybody the freedom to publish, it does mean that you might come across work that is of a poor standard or isn't ready for an edit. Independent authors can come from a variety of backgrounds. Some may be able to tell an excellent story, which is a real skill, but lack the education in or knowledge of punctuation or grammar to do it justice. Others may have a good grasp of the physical act of writing but struggle to pull their story together.

Tip

- Sometimes, an author's excitement can take over. There's an ethical line in the sand that you will have to draw between wanting to earn a living and not taking an author's money for a project that isn't ready for editing. If you spot massive problems with story structure or plot during your first read-through, then consider whether it's fair to the author to continue with a copyedit.

Teasing out the details of what an author needs and wants can take time and some long email exchanges. Many authors will approach an editor asking for a proofread, as this is the terminology they are most familiar with. In most cases, further intervention is required and as the expert it's up to you to explain to the client how you can help.

Independent authors aren't only those who plan to self-publish, either. Increasingly, authors are opting to have their work edited before sending it off to agents. You might also be asked to help edit synopses and query letters for submission packages.

It's worth delving a little into author motivation with a new client to find out what their plans and hopes are. An author who is planning to print five copies of their children's story for their grandchildren will have different needs from an author who is hoping their book will be the next Amazon bestseller. But both projects are equally deserving of good editing and a professional approach. You could include questions in your contact form to help you understand an author's goals, or send out a questionnaire when an author is interested in working with you.

3 | The bones of the story

Before a story is ready to be polished with a copyedit, it's essential that the basic building blocks are in place. Every book is different, but all good stories share some common elements. Being able to recognise when a story works on a foundation level – and being able to explain to the author what isn't quite working – can avoid situations where a client is left disappointed or facing negative reviews because there were major basic problems with their story.

In many respects, editing a poorly punctuated and spelled but gripping story is much easier than editing a very clean but turgid piece of prose. When approaching any project, be it from a publisher or an independent author, it's helpful to be able to recognise the warning signs that something isn't quite right with the bones of the story.

Plot

There's nothing worse than watching a gripping crime drama on TV and then, upon reaching the dénouement, realising you have no idea what's happened for the past half an hour. And so it is with books. Plots can be complex and multilayered, with many twists and turns, but the reader has to be able to follow the story all the way. Too many subplots or red herrings can leave a reader confused and flipping back through pages to see if they've missed something. If you as the editor are confused by a plot then a reader almost certainly will be, as editors tend to benefit from 'reading' a book in a shorter timeframe than an average reader. If you can't remember where you are in the plot after an overnight break of just 12 hours, then a reader who reads a couple of pages a night before bed twice a week will have no chance.

3 | The bones of the story

There are elements of a plot that an editor can look out for in order to best guide the author:

- Is there a satisfying ending?
- Are loose ends resolved?
- Can you pick out the beginning, middle and end?
- Does the ending make sense?
- Do all the elements of the story link together to ensure a smooth journey for the reader?

If the answer to any of these questions is no, it could be a sign that something is wrong with the author's plot. Often, asking them to provide a synopsis or a chapter-by-chapter outline of their story can pinpoint the problem. Sometimes an author may not realise that they've gone off-piste from their original plan, and asking them for an outline can put them back on track.

Finally, be on the lookout for *deus ex machina*; that is, solutions that magically appear out of thin air. Sometimes an author can lose their way and panic about pulling everything together for a satisfying ending. Instead of going back to the start and working out how to tie up the loose ends, they shoehorn in a person or item or situation that suddenly

resolves everything. If something feels too coincidental or convenient, it can leave a reader unsatisfied and irritated.

Scenes and structure

An author's chosen structure may be simple (writing the story in chronological order from start to finish) or complex (utilising flashbacks or hopping around in a story's timeline). Novice authors can find complex structural choices more difficult to get right – and this could lead to confusion in the reader. Writing in chronological order is more straightforward, and the writer will be less prone to pitfalls.

If an author has chosen to write something more complicated – say, a thriller with lots of 'parts', hopping back into the past as well as showing the reader the present – there are methods that can make this easier. The main thing to keep an eye out for is how an author is using scene and chapter breaks. If a chronological narrative is very frequently interrupted to explain events of the past, without any breaks, it's worth advising the author to consider a clearer separation. In thrillers, for instance, it's quite common to have chapters for 'then' and 'now', or to utilise chapters with specific date headings. This is a much clearer structure that signals to the reader where they are in the timeline, avoiding a confusing or jerky reading experience.

In a chronological narrative, watch out for any scenes that don't mesh well with the rest, and events that feel random. Some novels contain lots of 'filler' scenes, and this is often because the author hasn't threaded in a solid sense of cause and effect to weave scenes and events together. If many scenes appear to be detached from the overarching plot, readers will be left wondering about the purpose of the story.

Conflict and tension

All stories have conflict – otherwise, reading wouldn't be any fun! There aren't many novels where characters just go about their day, from brushing their teeth to going to work and sleeping, without much else happening in between. There would be no tension and drama to enjoy.

Conflict and tension need to be purposeful and clearly linked to the main plot. When an author includes lots of random events to add drama, but they aren't connected to the story's purpose, we get what is known as 'false tension'. For example, think about *The Hunger Games*. The point of the story is that Katniss volunteers for a battle-to-the-death in place of her sister, and the story's events therefore focus on her preparing for and taking part in the Games. But if we had two hundred pages of Katniss travelling to the Games on foot, and dealing with other problems, such as being attacked by random groups of bandits or bullies who never show up again, or breaking her leg by stumbling over a rock, that would be false tension.

Point of view

Point of view is a perennial sticking point with authors both novice and experienced. There are many books written on point of view alone, and it often trips up the unwary author. Problems with point of view can be difficult to nail down. Often, a reader is just left with a vague sense that something isn't right or that they don't feel engaged with the story. This can happen when point of view is inconsistent; for example, in a story written almost entirely from the perspective of a streetwise detective, it suddenly appears from the perspective of his elderly aunt instead. That kind of thing can throw a reader for a loop.

There's a term that's commonly used to denote rapid or repeated changes of point of view without scene breaks or other vehicles to show the shift in perspective: head-hopping. But recognising head-hopping as opposed to just an omniscient narrator or distant third-person view can be very difficult, and it's rarely black and white. Skilled authors can handle point of view transitions seamlessly; novice authors can sometimes jump from deep in one character's head to deep into another's without giving the reader a chance to adjust. Some authors are also very skilled at writing multiple points of view. For example, Elizabeth Jane Howard in her *Cazalet Chronicles*, or Samantha Shannon in *The Priory of the Orange Tree*. Multiple points of view in the same

chapter (so long as they're broken up with scene breaks) can work well, but jarring changes that pull you out of the story, such as head-hopping regularly within a scene, should be avoided. Alongside this, be on the lookout for passages where you can't work out whose head you're in or where the point of view character suddenly sees themselves externally (such as noting that their face looks like a tomato when they aren't looking in a mirror).

Pace

We've all read books that have dragged ... and dragged ... and dragged. Books where nothing seems to happen for chapter upon chapter have problems with pacing. This is often due to inexperienced authors trying to shoehorn in as much backstory about characters and situations as they can instead of letting scenes play out organically and drip-feeding the information to readers more gradually (or just trusting readers to read between the lines and make their own judgements).

A good indicator of a slowing pace is when you're faced with several pages of narrative with no dialogue. This is often a sign of info-dumping, where instead of active scenes with characters taking part in the story, you have long portions of explanation and exposition. These are the pages readers tend to flick past to get to the good stuff.

If a story seems to be dragging, it's worth asking: Is this information necessary? And does the story start in the right place? While this might sound strange, it's quite common for authors to begin a story too early.

> ### Tip
> - Sometimes, cutting out the first couple of chapters and starting with the first real 'event' can improve the pace. If your attention starts to flag while reading or editing, note this down for the author.

Characterisation

Characters are paramount to the development of a story. Some genres focus more on character development than others. For example, plot-driven books like thrillers or adventure stories tend to have less of a focus on character relationships and growth than works of literary fiction or romance. But regardless of genre, characters should be believable. They should also be flawed. Perfect characters don't endear themselves to anyone. Readers want to relate to characters, not be irritated by them.

Characters should also have clear motivations – if a reader is unclear what a character's goal is, then their narrative arc will end up being unsatisfying. Likewise, if a character has no conflict, be it external or internal, then there's nothing pushing that character to grow and evolve.

> *A character doesn't have to be likeable. Sometimes even protagonists can be quite unlikeable, as in* Gone Girl. *But it is important that there is a reason for their behaviour and that the reader understands why they act in the way they do.*

It's also important that characters behave consistently. A mild-mannered middle-aged man is unlikely to stab someone to death out of the blue unless there's more going on beneath the surface. Sometimes, inconsistency is key to the story and essential to the plot. Think about how the characters are behaving based on their previous experiences and reactions, and make a note of anything that seems off. If the inconsistency doesn't seem important on a broader scale later, it may need to be changed.

When it comes to protagonists, it's best to avoid passivity. Passive protagonists often read like sidekicks, rather than being the focal point, because they don't take charge and drive the story themselves. If an author's protagonist lacks a goal, doesn't have any motivation or drive, and if solutions and actions are often assigned to other characters, you're dealing with a passive protagonist. It may be that the author has chosen the wrong protagonist for the story – or they may just need to revise to make this character more active, and the one with the major goal.

Showing vs telling

'Show, don't tell' is an oft-repeated phrase to writers and refers to avoiding too much exposition, aka telling. And it's usually good advice. Showing the reader that a character is violent, such as a scene where he breaks someone's nose, is much stronger than just writing 'David was a violent man'. But as with all things fiction, there's a balance to be found. An author can go too far and become too concerned with showing, making everything into overblown scenes and losing track of the pace of the story.

Sometimes, it's fine to tell. The real challenge is judging whether an author has got the balance right. Are there pieces of information relayed to the reader that could be related in a different way, perhaps in a scene or in a piece of dialogue between characters? Are there long pieces of narrative with lots of information about characters or events? If so, it might be worth suggesting to the author that they readdress the show vs tell balance.

Dialogue

Dialogue is the lifeblood of a novel. When you pick up a book in a bookshop and flick through, you are probably unconsciously taking note of how much white space there is. White space = dialogue. No white space = a lot of narrative.

But it's not enough just to have characters talking to each other. Their dialogue should be realistic in the sense that it should reflect how that specific character would speak. For example, a teenager is unlikely to use very formal language or avoid contractions. But it also shouldn't be too realistic – dialogue peppered with heavy accents, umms and aahs, throat-clearing and other verbal tics is difficult to read. Less is usually more.

Dialogue should be punchy. Every word should fight for its space on the page. And beware long monologues. In conversations, people don't generally speak for five minutes without any input from the other person (unless you get very unlucky at a party). Someone explaining their dastardly plot without pause or interruption for two or three pages will very quickly become unbelievable. Characters should generally have conversations, not give speeches.

And finally, look out for 'talking heads'. Dialogue needs to be balanced with the other considerations of the scene, such as location and the actions of those taking part in the conversation. Two people talking at each other with no indication of what they are doing or where they are for pages and pages on end is known as 'talking heads syndrome'. Essentially, the characters have been reduced to heads, yapping back and forward at each other, without any link to the scene or the story around them.

Tense times

Next to point of view, getting tenses right is the thing that trips novice authors up the most. It's not uncommon for them to waver back and forward, changing their book from past to present and back to past again, leaving lots of inconsistencies to clean up.

Most stories are told in simple past tense, but present tense is common in certain genres, particularly young adult, thrillers and romance. It's the marmite of fiction – some people refuse to read present tense; others really enjoy the immediacy of it. The challenge with present tense is to prevent a story sounding like a running commentary on someone's life – 'I go to the fridge. I open it. I take out some cheese ...'.

> **Tip**
> - It's often worth pointing out to authors that choosing present tense will be noticeable, while going with simple past tense won't. Not wanting to rock the boat isn't necessarily a valid reason to abandon present tense, but if an author isn't sure or is struggling to decide, it might be helpful for them to know that present tense tends to attract more criticism.

Whatever tense an author settles on, it's important that it is consistent throughout. (Although note that sometimes an author will choose a tense for the main narrative but then use another tense to denote flashback or premonition scenes. As long as this remains consistent and clear, there is usually no problem with this approach.)

Author voice

Author voice and style are incredibly important when editing fiction: If you think about your own favourite authors, their unique voice is what makes their writing so enjoyable. It can be difficult sometimes to separate what you would do from what the author has done, particularly if you think your way is better. And sometimes there's no harm in offering alternatives.

Always keep in your head that this isn't your book – it's your client's, and their choice of language and style is a hallmark of their writing and their own personal 'brand'.

It's more difficult when working with authors who are still developing their voice. First-time authors might waver between their own voice and a more generic style of writing. They might even slip into the voice of their own favourite author from time to time. Editing with empathy can help tease out the author's voice, and spotting when they have strayed from the path or got themselves in a muddle can help keep their voice consistent across the whole book.

Series

When dealing with a series, it's important to evaluate every book on its own merit. Even if a book is part of a trilogy, where the story develops, each book should have a satisfying arc within it. Cliffhangers can be exciting, but a reader will be left annoyed if nothing is resolved in book one and they have to wait months or years for book two or book three.

The usual structure for a trilogy is to have a narrative arc that stretches over the three books, with smaller, interweaving arcs in the individual books that offer the reader some sense of satisfaction. If you think about the *Lord of the Rings* trilogy, for example, each book has its own arc that fits into the wider storyline.

When working on series that involve the same character but in different stories, such as a detective series, it's important to track the character's development and make sure they are growing in some way – and ensure their behaviour makes sense given the books that have come before. A character might react very differently in book seven to a scenario that also happened in book one, thanks to an incident that happened in book four.

> **Tip**
> - It can be useful to create what's known as a 'story bible' when working on a series. This is a document that holds crucial pieces of information pulled from each book. This can include locations and settings, character descriptions, relationships, important events, timeline details, history and bits of world-building information.

A story bible is different to a style sheet in the sense that it may hold some similar information, but the focus is less on keeping track of editorial and stylistic choices, and more on avoiding plot-, world- or character-based errors across the series. Story bibles can include things like maps, illustrations, timelines, family trees and notes on magic systems or fictional technology. For example, in a novel with a complex family tree, you don't want a second cousin in book one suddenly becoming a third cousin in book four; you also want to make sure the world-building rules remain consistent. Sometimes, authors will supply their own story bible and you can expand upon it. If not, creating one can help you as you work across multiple books in a series.

> *Always keep in your head that this isn't your book – it's your client's.*

4 | Copyediting

Once the structure of a novel is in good shape, the editor's focus can turn to the language. You might have heard the phrase that there are 'no rules' when it comes to fiction. This isn't quite true – there are still rules, or rather conventions, but they tend to be looser and more open to interpretation.

While this might sound quite freeing, particularly if you have been working on material with very strict guidelines, it does bring an element of uncertainty with it. Sometimes you have to trust your editor's ear instead of relying on the security of a style guide or dictionary. Sometimes you and the author will be at odds over what is a 'mistake' and what is a genuine style choice.

Who you are working for will have some bearing on your handling of the text too. Publishers often have their own style guides and can be quite rigid, but when working with a self-publisher, they might not have

the knowledge to distinguish an egregious error from what is simply a non-standard use of language that helps to tell their story. By the time a manuscript reaches your inbox for copyediting (or desk, although editing on paper is increasingly rare these days), you shouldn't have to worry about things like pacing, plot or characterisation. But inevitably, as you read through, you will find a few things that need to be flagged or queried.

How you approach the manuscript when you receive it is up to you. Some editors like to read through the manuscript entirely without making any changes to get a feel for the author's style and get a handle on the plot and characters. Other editors prefer to jump in and start editing straight away without being influenced by any knowledge of what happens. Neither way is more valid than the other. Sometimes the budget might preclude doing a read-through before editing, but sometimes a complex story would benefit from a thorough read before the editing begins. You might change your approach depending on the manuscript itself. The important thing is that you are comfortable.

Whether you're a dive-in-and-start kind of editor or a sit-back-and-consider kind, the issues you face will be the same.

Style sheets

Style sheets are of huge importance when working on fiction. They tend to be more comprehensive than non-fiction style sheets, simply because fiction has a lot of elements where consistency is important. Even if you are working for an independent author who can't afford a separate proofread, creating a style sheet is an important part of the editing process. Make sure the author gets a copy too; it'll help them for future novels or if they do eventually get their current manuscript proofread.

Many editors create a template for style sheets that they can then adapt for each new project. Aside from the usual concerns such as spellings and how to handle punctuation, a fiction style sheet might include information on character appearance and backstory, a timeline, a note of the geographical locations in the story, details of any lore or world-building rules in fantasy or science fiction novels, and notes on how you've formatted the manuscript. It's important to tailor your style sheet to the needs of each project. You might even want to include some information for clients on how to handle your edits. Some authors might be unfamiliar with how to use Word's Track Changes feature and would benefit from guidance on how to accept and reject changes or how to respond to queries.

Timelines

Time has no meaning when you're engrossed in a good book. Unfortunately, time can also behave peculiarly within a book's pages. Problems with timelines are incredibly common and can vary from minor hiccups to major, plot-altering problems.

> **Tip**
> - It can be useful to keep a timeline, noting down whenever a time of day, day of the week, month, year or other information relating to chronology is mentioned. This can help you spot minor problems such as a character going to work seven days in a row or children going to school on a Saturday.

Occasionally, timeline problems can have much bigger impacts on the plot. For example, a romance novel in which February passes by without a mention of Valentine's Day would probably make some readers confused and/or dissatisfied. And in a police procedural, getting the time or date of a crime wrong could make the entire plot unravel.

It's easy to fall into the trap of wondering if a reader will really notice if a certain date ten years ago is mentioned as a Wednesday when in reality it was a Thursday. While it might seem a random date to you and not one you would remember, it could easily be an important date to a reader, such as the date their child was born, or the day they started a new job. If in doubt, check dates and days all line up and if they don't, query the author. Be careful when changing dates and times as they might have a knock-on effect on the rest of the novel – always leave a comment for the author so they can cross-check any changes with the rest of their story.

Consistency

Staying consistent over 80,000 words or more can be difficult for an author, particularly if they have changed character names and details many times during the self-editing process. Keeping careful notes on character details is essential for spotting problems like changing eye or hair colours, someone driving an Audi one week and a BMW the next or a hairdresser becoming a bank manager.

Look out for the changing interiors of houses too. The TV series *Friends* came in for light-hearted criticism for the occasional rearranging of Monica and Rachel's apartment, so be sure to note down when a room layout is mentioned. You might even want to draw a map just for your own information.

One thing to watch for is characters whose names are styled in different ways throughout – for example, a character called variously Jennifer, Jen and Jenny in narrative. While different characters might well call her by different names, in the narrative it's generally best to stick to one name for consistency.

Punctuating dialogue

Even experienced authors can struggle with the correct way to punctuate dialogue. New speakers should get a new line, and when dialogue from the same speaker is split over several paragraphs, the usual convention is to leave the end of the paragraph open but start the next with an open quote mark.

The usage of dialogue tags and action beats can trip authors up. It's quite common for words such as 'smiled' or 'sighed' to be used as dialogue tags. While strictly speaking people can't really smile or sigh sentences, some publishers don't mind this usage, so it's often a judgement call over whether to allow them. Just make sure that action beats and tags are punctuated appropriately:

> *'I am going to the shop,' he said.*

> *'I am going to the shop.' He stomped away furiously.*

For interrupted speech, it's common to use an en (–) or an em (—) dash to signify the interruption:

> *'I'm going to—'*

When speech is punctuated with an action in the middle, you can use the parentheses style used elsewhere in the book.

> *'It's not fair that you' – he looked at David angrily – 'get to go and I don't!'*

Note that the dashes are used outside the quoted material as they belong to the action, not the dialogue (unlike an interruption). Publishing houses may have their own preferences for styling speech where an action takes place in the middle of the dialogue (such as using commas within the quotation marks instead). If you're working with a publisher, they will usually provide their own house style covering these preferences.

Use ellipses (…) to indicate when speech trails off or someone is uncertain. And if someone is stammering, hyphens between letters (eg 'I-I-I-I'm sorry') are usually sufficient (but as mentioned previously, less is usually more with this kind of thing).

Take particular care when letters are omitted to show a character is speaking in an accent – Word generally puts the apostrophe the wrong way round. It should be: **come 'ere**, not **'ere**.

Finally, be mindful of punctuation when editing 'speech within speech'. For example, if a character is talking to another character and quoting something that someone else said, you want to place that in quotation marks as well. If dialogue throughout the novel is in double quotation marks, any quotes within dialogue should be in single quotation marks. Here's an example:

> "I was over at Emily's house, and her mum stormed right up to me and said, 'Get out. I don't want you coming here again after what happened last time.' Can you believe that?"

Inner monologue and thoughts

There are various ways to punctuate or illustrate inner monologue and/or thoughts, and a lot of the time it comes down to the context. If the narrative is in very close first person, you might find that there's no need to mark thoughts as such – it's already clear that these are the thoughts of the first-person character. Sometimes a character's thoughts can take on a different form from the rest of the book, however. For example, a third-person point of view story might occasionally have the protagonist speaking to themselves in first person: *What are you doing, Katherine?!* In this case, it's sometimes helpful to use italics to denote the shift as otherwise the reader could become confused.

A general rule of thumb is to choose the option that creates the least narrative distance – that is, don't use italics and a 'he thought' tag when just italics will do. And if you can get away without using either, then it's probably good to do so.

Fact-checking

Getting the right balance of fact-checking is tricky. With some novels, it's all too easy to go down the rabbit hole and spend hours checking every fact, no matter how obscure. However, it's unlikely your budget will allow for the time it takes to check every little detail. You can often get a feel for how well researched something is if you verify the first five or six facts you come across. If everything checks out, then you might feel comfortable only checking things that stick out to you or that can be easily verified. If your budget is very tight, you don't even need to check them – sometimes leaving a comment saying 'Please check this is accurate' serves the purpose.

Difficulties can arise when you are working on something laden with facts, usually historical fiction, and you notice that there's a recurring problem. Authors writing historical fiction should have done their research, but if you notice more than the odd dodgy fact, then it might be time to go back to your client or the publisher and explain your concerns. Editors can't be experts in every genre and period of history and can't be expected to spot every factual error, but if you can quickly check things like the time it takes to drive between two areas, or what day of the week 1 March 1987 was, then it's often worth doing.

Anachronisms

Some anachronisms are easily spotted. Someone texting their friend in the 1980s, for example, would immediately jump out. However, others are a lot more subtle. For example, reference being made to Superman in a story set in Britain in the late 1930s. The character was only introduced in America in 1938, so it would be unlikely to be a household name in Britain that same year.

Some of these things are easily checked. Others, such as phrases and pop culture references, require a bit more work. As with fact-checking, if your budget doesn't allow for spending time on research, it can be worth just flagging dubious phrases and references and asking the author to verify these were in use when the story is set.

There's also an argument to be made about accuracy versus readability when dealing with stories set way back in history. Writing dialogue for characters in ancient Egypt has to be understandable and accessible for a modern audience, so there is some leeway here. Likewise, characters in the Middle Ages should be authentic in the sense that they don't use modern phrases, but the author can take some liberties in the interests of making them understandable for a modern reader.

Avoiding over-correction

Sometimes a mistake is just a mistake. But sometimes, a 'mistake' may have been made intentionally for the purposes of the writing. Comma splices get quite a bad rap, but they are very much part of some writers' styles (see Kate Atkinson's books as an example).

Tip
- Use your own judgement to evaluate whether something has been done for effect or whether it's just a mistake or oversight. Comma splices, for example, can often be used to good effect in speech or internal monologue for giving an anxious, breathless feel to a piece of writing. Likewise, unusual grammar in speech can be important for characterisation, and correcting it could change the author's character in a way they don't want.

When making changes, always be aware of how they will affect the surrounding text and what effect your change will have. If in doubt, leave a comment to explain and let the author decide.

Unlike other forms of editing (such as editing academic materials), fiction editing requires more flexibility when it comes to breaking the 'rules', but it's still important to think about whether this creative choice works with the text. For example, Cormac McCarthy may have been able to avoid using quotation marks in *The Road*, but a beginning writer might struggle to pull this off well.

Repetition and redundancy

As you're working on a manuscript, you may come across words and phrases that the author has used repetitively. If done too frequently, this can pull the reader out of the story and disrupt the flow of the narrative. These types of corrections usually fall under heavier editing (a line edit or a heavy copyedit). You're likely to need to deal with this more frequently when working with authors independently, but sometimes publishers do request that copyeditors watch for certain repeated words. Common culprits include 'very', 'really', 'that', 'but', 'just', 'suddenly', 'at that moment', and filter words such as 'he saw', 'she heard', 'they felt' and so on.

Authors may also fall into using redundant language, or repeating redundant descriptions. These are often things like eye-related descriptions (describing where a character is looking too often, or overusing words like 'gaze', 'eye', 'stare' and 'look'), and describing body parts when it's unnecessary to do so ('she pulled the door open with her hand' as opposed to 'she pulled the door open').

Use your discretion when trimming these down. These words and phrases aren't things to be avoided at all times, of course, but if your author is overusing them and you've agreed on a heavier edit, you can offer suggested changes and solutions or cut them down. If you're only performing a light copyedit with minimal intervention, though, you'll need to exercise restraint and leave well enough alone.

Dealing with numbers

Common sense is the most important consideration when dealing with numbers. Fiction tends to favour spelling out numbers wherever possible, so ages (thirty-five) and simple numbers (three hundred, two thousand, etc) are usually spelled out. For more complicated numbers (such as £2,568.98) or things like phone numbers, numerals are usually more sensible. In addition, numerals are often used when the subject is much more recognisable in numerical form – for example, 999 and 24/7.

For times of day, go with consistency – 10am is fine, as is ten o'clock. Sometimes genre and context will help you decide. For example, in a military thriller or a crime novel with a very important or precise timeline, 24-hour clock might be more appropriate.

If in doubt, you can also consult style guides such as *New Hart's Rules* for UK English and *The Chicago Manual of Style* for US English. When working with publishing houses, they will most likely want you to adhere to a particular style guide, or to follow their own house style, unless they are happy to go with the author's choice, provided it's consistent.

Copyright and legal concerns

Particularly when working with self-publishers, you might feel uncomfortable about the inclusion of copyrighted material or the use of real people and products. If you have any concerns whatsoever, advise your author to seek advice from a lawyer.

Use of real places (such as Starbucks, Asda, etc) can add authenticity to a novel and there is usually no issue with using them to set the scene. However, if you have a story where the owner of a well-known restaurant chain turns out to be a serial killer who is feeding his customers parts of his victims, that's another case entirely, and the restaurant in question should be changed to a fictional one.

Likewise, using real products (iPhones, Porsches, etc) is fine, unless the author's story is making unverified claims about their safety or similar.

It's fine to have a character use their iPhone to make a call; it's not fine to have a story where iPhones are secretly being used by the government to record everything we do. Authors might also want to reference or use real people, such as celebrities or public figures, in their books. This tends to be more common in genres like historical fiction, where, for instance, characters might encounter a long-dead historical figure like Jane Austen or William Shakespeare. Using people who are alive today opens up a big legal can of worms – and even using long-deceased people in fiction can be risky, particularly if they have a literary estate or living family members. Again, in this case, you can recommend that your author seek legal advice before going ahead with this.

Authors sometimes want to use song lyrics in their novels, but they can be notoriously difficult to get consent for. Given the short length of most songs, some argue that even one line or the title constitutes a significant portion and can't be considered 'fair dealing'. Using song lyrics can quickly become an expensive business so it's always worth leaving an author query suggesting they seek consent, unless the song is an old nursery rhyme or something of that nature, where there is no copyrighted writer (but even that must be certain). Works in the public domain are usually fine to use, but authors should double check that they have the right to use these works.

More recently, there has been a lot of debate about advancing technology such as AI and copyright. This is an ever-changing and fast-growing area. Be mindful that anything fed into an AI system may be seen by whoever created that system, so unlike efficiency tools, it may be ill-advised to feed client work into these systems, which would breach client confidentiality.

Some writers are now opting to use AI in their own writing – it's up to you whether you decide to take on these projects. There is growing debate and speculation around the data the AI learns from being pulled from existing literary works, which may also raise copyright concerns. If you receive a project from an author and are in any doubt about the use of AI, you can always ask them for more details and recommend they get legal advice.

Genre concerns

Sometimes specific genres have their own particular tropes and conventions and it's useful to be aware of these. In romance fiction, for example, you might come across slightly unusual dialogue tags (such as 'gritted' or 'ground out'). These are quite common in romance novels but might attract a greater degree of censure if they were included in a crime novel, for example. In science fiction, it's quite common to capitalise specific terms and made-up words where you might not do so otherwise.

This is where it's useful, particularly when working with individuals who don't have a style guide to offer, to keep abreast of the industry and read different genres so you are up to date with changes in publishing conventions. If in doubt, Amazon's Look Inside feature will allow you to see a few pages inside books of a similar genre – this can sometimes be useful for seeing how specific points are styled. You can also get free samples of all Kindle books. And don't neglect the books on your own shelves if you want to see how other editors and publishers have chosen to handle certain things.

Target audience

As with genre, certain age categories have particular conventions and expectations attached to them. When copyediting a manuscript, keep in mind the target audience of the project, and watch for anything that

doesn't fit. For example, swearing or extreme violence in a middle grade book is best left out, unless the author wants to prompt angry reviews from parents!

You probably won't need to keep an eye on this when working with publishers (who will have already provided their authors with some guidance during the developmental stage), but independent authors – particularly if they are new to writing for a particular age category – may need more help.

If you're interested in working on certain age categories such as middle grade or young adult (YA) books, but aren't overly familiar with them, the best way to learn is by reading lots of books in those categories. Young adult tends to have slightly more flexibility when it comes to content, compared to middle grade and younger. You can also read craft books on writing and editing children's books to develop your knowledge.

Conscious language

Conscious language, or inclusive language, is about using language mindfully and intentionally. Certain language choices might appear to be biased, disrespectful or contribute to stereotypes and stigma – in fiction, for example, all of the female characters might be defined superficially by their appearance, or the author might have frequently used slurs in the narrative to describe particular groups of people based on their race, ethnicity, sexual orientation, disability and so on.

Conscious language isn't about suppressing what an author is trying to say, or their vision, but encouraging thoughtfulness around context, intent and the readership to determine whether changes might be necessary. Be on the lookout for any unintentionally stigmatising or biased language and highlight this for the author so they can consider what to do. You could also recommend that an author hire a specialist reader, known as a sensitivity, diversity or authenticity reader, particularly if they're writing outside their own experience and need additional help.

Document formatting

If you're working for a publisher, the manuscript might be supplied with a Word template already applied or that you can apply yourself. This means that all you need to do is follow their guidelines for applying styles to the various headings.

In other cases, publishers might ask you to 'tag' or 'code' the different elements of the manuscript yourself, and they will provide you with guidelines for how they prefer this to be done. Square brackets are common; for example, the different elements of a manuscript might be styled like this:

[CN]Chapter One[/CN] for a chapter number
[CH]Alice[/CH] for an un-numbered chapter heading
[LINE BREAK]
[START TEXT MESSAGE] [/END TEXT MESSAGE]

When working for an independent author, though, you'll often find that the document is in need of formatting before you begin work. Often, authors just open Word and start writing with whatever the default settings are. Or they might be using another program such as Scrivener to write their draft, which when opened in Word brings with it lots of unwanted formatting. There might be odd typefaces, different sizes of text, unclear chapter headings, extra spaces, tabs instead of indents, etc. It's worth spending a bit of time getting the document into a workable state to begin editing.

First of all, it's a good idea to run some basic searches to get rid of things like multiple spaces. This is easily done by opening the Find and Replace box, entering two spaces in the Find box and entering one space in the Replace box. Repeat this until it stops finding results. You can also do similar for getting rid of extra lines between paragraphs by entering ^p^p in the Find box, and ^p in the Replace box.

You can then either attach your own template that you've made previously with your own options for indents and heading styles, or amend the client's style to be more workable. For example, you'll probably want to increase line spacing in the 'Normal' style to make the document easier to work on, as well as give chapter headings their own style so you can use the navigation pane to move around the document. You'll also want to remove tabs and set up the Normal style to have indents instead.

Bear in mind that many independent authors plan to format their documents for print or ebook themselves. It's important you can provide as clean a document as possible to minimise the things that can go wrong at the layout stage. Applying heading styles or Word templates can still be useful to help the author identify the different areas of the manuscript when they come to do their own formatting – or to signal these to a formatter or typesetter if the author will be hiring one.

Efficiency tools

Efficiency tools are useful for fiction editing because they can help you to save time and speed up tasks that might otherwise take you an incredibly long time. Not only can they help you edit more efficiently, but they can assist you in streamlining your business overall as well.

Macros

Macros are one of the biggest time-savers around when editing in Word. Macros are automated tasks that run in Word to perform various functions. Some macros make changes, others simply highlight words or phrases and let you decide what to change, and others analyse the document and display results separately. They might seem intimidating to begin with and you might protest that you don't know anything about code, but you don't need to.

There's no need to reinvent the wheel – most things you'll want to do will already have been done by someone else. And that someone else is more likely than not to be CIEP member Paul Beverley, who has a free downloadable tome of macros specifically for editors.

Some of the best macros for fiction editors are his Chronology Checker (this can help you put together a timeline), ProperNounAlyse (invaluable for spotting differently spelled place names and character names) and various macros for making common punctuation changes (such as switching a full stop for a comma in dialogue and vice versa).

In most cases, it's just a case of copying and pasting the source code and then running the macro – no coding or programming knowledge is needed.

Add-ins

The Word add-in PerfectIt is also great for checking consistency on book-length manuscripts, and you can set up your own style sheets to enforce publisher style rules or your own.

There are also other programs, such as EditTools and Editor's Toolkit, that automate various parts of the clean-up process to increase your efficiency.

Text expanders

Text expander tools can save you time and energy – you can set them up to automatically insert an often-used query to an author or a long section of text that you need regularly (such as an explanation you find yourself needing to give to multiple writers). Instead of having to copy and paste a chunk of text you've kept ready in a separate Word document, you can input all your commonly used queries and explanations into the text expander, and use a quick, assigned keystroke to input that text. You can use these for all manner of things, from leaving author queries to adding style sheet information.

Many text expander services offer a free version if you only need a small amount of input, or you can pay for more comprehensive tools and more input. Some of the most commonly used are PhraseExpress (for Mac, with a very good free option) and TextExpander (Windows and Mac).

5 | Resources

Books

Ackerman, Angela and Puglisi, Becca (2012). *The Emotion Thesaurus: A Writer's Guide to Character Expression*.

Bickham, Jack M (1993). *Scene & Structure*. Writer's Digest Books, US.

Brody, Jessica (2018). *Save the Cat! Writes a Novel*. Ten Speed Press, California.

Brody, Jessica (2023). *Save the Cat! Writes a Young Adult Novel*. Ten Speed Press, California.

Browne, Renni and King, Dave (2004). *Self-Editing for Fiction Writers*. 2nd edition. New York: HarperCollins.

Chester, Deborah (2016). *The Fantasy Fiction Formula*. Manchester University Press, Manchester.

Gardner, John (2001). *The Art of Fiction*. New York: Vintage.

Hill, Beth (2016). *The Magic of Fiction: Crafting Words into Story: The Writer's Guide to Writing & Editing*. Title Page Books.

King, Stephen (2001). *On Writing*. London: New English Library.

Klein, Cheryl B (2016). *The Magic Words: Writing Great Books for Children and Young Adults*. W. W. Norton & Company, Inc., New York.

Newman, Sandra & Mittelmark, Howard (2009). *How Not to Write a Novel*. London: Penguin.

Noble, William (1987). *'Shut UP!' He Explained: A Writer's Guide to the Uses and Misuses of Dialogue*. California: The Write Thought.

Rasley, Alicia (2008). *The Power of Point of View: Make Your Story Come to Life*. Devon: David & Charles.

Schneider, Amy J (2023). *The Chicago Guide to Copyediting Fiction*. The University of Chicago Press, Chicago.

Sjoholm, Barbara (2010). *An Editor's Guide to Working with Authors*. Port Townsend, WA: Rainforest Press.

Weiland, KM (2013). *Structuring Your Novel: Essential Keys for Writing an Outstanding Story*. PenForASword.

Blogs and websites

In no particular order ...

Helping Writers become Authors, KM Weiland's blog on different aspects of craft: **www.helpingwritersbecomeauthors.com**.

Writers' and Artists' Yearbook, the writer's bible, also has a very helpful website: **writersandartists.co.uk**.

The Literary Consultancy is an excellent writers' advisory service run by publishing professionals; its website includes an invaluable FAQs page: **literaryconsultancy.co.uk**.

The Alliance of Independent Authors (ALLi) provides support and advice for authors and has a Partner Directory where editors can advertise services: **allianceindependentauthors.org**.

Author Emma Darwin's blog on writing fiction: **emmadarwin.typepad.com/thisitchofwriting**.

Beth Hill's blog (a US fiction editor): **theeditorsblog.net**.

Jane Friedman's resources for authors: **janefriedman.com/resources**.

5 | Resources

A popular and active online writing community: **writewords.org.uk**.

Tips for writers and editors on the Writer's Digest website: **writersdigest.com**.

Sophie Playle has useful articles for authors and editors: **liminalpages.com/blog**.

Kia Thomas' blog for authors and editors: **kiathomasediting.com/blog**.

Louise Harnby has a huge library of resources for editors and authors: **louiseharnbyproofreader.com**.

US editor Lisa Poisso's blog: **lisapoisso.com/category/clarity-tools-and-skills-forauthors**.

Paul Beverley's huge collection of macros: **archivepub.co.uk/book.html**.

Rachel Rowlands' blog on fiction writing craft, editing and publishing: **rachelrowlands.com/blog**.

Writing with Color, a useful advice page on writing diversely: **writingwithcolor.tumblr.com**.

The Conscious Style Guide, a resource for writers and editors on conscious language: **consciousstyleguide.com**.

6 | Glossary

Action beats – Character actions used in lieu of dialogue tags – 'I'm so angry.' He slammed the door behind him.

Conflict – The thing(s) preventing the protagonist from achieving their goals. Conflict can be internal and/or external.

Dialogue – A conversation between characters or one character speaking, usually enclosed in quotation marks.

Dialogue tags – A word or phrase that attributes a piece of speech, such as 'asked', 'said', 'whispered'.

Exposition – A comprehensive description and explanation of an idea or theory.

False tension – Tension that feels manufactured and detached from the overarching story or hook, rather than being organically built into the story.

Head-hopping – When point of view jumps rapidly from character to character in a scene.

Inner monologue – A character's innermost thoughts when they talk directly to themselves.

Motivation – The reason for a character's actions throughout a novel.

Narrative arc – The structure and shape of a story – a basic arc consists of a beginning, middle and end.

Narrative distance – How close (or distant) the reader feels to the narrator, characters or other elements in a story.

Narrator – The character who tells or explains a story or describes what is happening.

Pacing – The speed and rhythm of a story; how quickly the events unfold.

Plot – The heart of the story, ie what happens, how and why.

Point of view (POV) – The perspective from which a story is told. First-person POV is when a story is told from the direct perspective of generally one character using the pronouns 'I' and 'me'. Third-person is when a story is told from the POV of one or more characters using the pronouns 'he/she' and 'him/her'. Omniscient is a story with an all-seeing narrator or character who knows what other characters are thinking or feeling.

Talking heads – Dialogue that goes back and forth between characters with few or no dialogue tags or action beats and little sense of scene.

About the authors

Katherine Trail is a former newspaper chief subeditor who specialised in editing fiction, mainly for independent authors and small publishers. She is a former Advanced Professional Member of the CIEP and is based in Aberdeenshire.

Rachel Rowlands is a fiction editor, author and Advanced Professional Member of the CIEP. She has a degree in English and Creative Writing and has worked on hundreds of books for both independent authors and publishing houses, including Hachette, HarperCollins, Black Library, Canelo and Penguin Random House.

racheljrowlands.com

Acknowledgements

With thanks to the CIEP Information Team and the following CIEP members who reviewed the draft of this guide and provided helpful advice and comments.

Averill Buchanan, **averillbuchanan.com**

Katherine Swailes, **writeorwrong.co.nz**

Helen Bleck, **editingforwriters.com**

www.ingramcontent.com/pod-product-compliance
Lightning Source LLC
Chambersburg PA
CBHW041315110526
44591CB00022B/2919